To the Honorable Schuyler Colfax,
*Speaker of the House of Representatives:*

My attention has been called to the defence of Gen. Butler before the House of Representatives, in relation to the New Orleans gold. That defence, as published in the *Globe*, I propose to review, and leave you to say whether it is not an audacious sham which ought to be exposed.

I am entirely certain that the very eminent and honorable gentleman who conducted the defence fully believed that it was fairly made, and that there was a full, honest, and just exposition of the whole case. But he has been entirely misled, and Samuel Smith & Co., my clients, have suffered great injustice thereby. The counsel of Gen. Butler commences his defence of that gold transaction by reading a letter from Mr. Rufus Wapples, dated May 12th, 1864. The letter says:—"*As I left the city (New Orleans) soon after the commencement of hostilities, and staid in Washington city till May of last year, I cannot speak from personal knowledge.*"

Says Mr. Boutwell, "I have caused that to be read as "furnishing *a basis in evidence* for the seizure of the money "in question."

As the gold was taken a little more than two years before, and as Mr. Wapples admits that he was not in New Orleans, but in Washington, and knows nothing whatever upon the subject himself, "that *basis in evidence*" looks a little "shaky." The *structure* was built two years before "*the basis*" was laid. The foundation has not even the firmness of moving sand, it is "airy nothing." A structure upon such a base will be likely to tumble, and somebody will "*get hurt*" in the ruins.

In the New York Court of Common Pleas the case of Samuel Smith & Co., agst. Benjamin F. Butler, will soon come on before the Court and a jury. Many living witnesses will be examined, and new documentary evidence will be produced. I bespeak your attention to that trial; the proceedings will not be drowsy reading. Meanwhile, let me briefly review the case presented by General Butler before the House. My excuse for this apparent intrusion is that I am Mr. Smith's counsel, and from him Gen. Butler took $50,000 in gold, and has kept it himself through a period of two years and nine months, although Mr. Smith, by his counsel, proposed in writing simply that Gen. Butler "pay over the money to the War Office or "to the Treasury, and leave me to such remedy there as "the Government may think fit," which reasonable propositions continued never accepted, but evaded and declined, until the 26th of last October, when the counsel wrote to the General—"You leave Mr. Smith no alternative but to "commence an action." General Butler, in his letter of the 28th of March, 1864, excuses himself thus for not paying over this money:—"When I settled my accounts at the War Office, the question of what should be done with this money of Samuel Smith & Co. came under discussion, and I then said to the Secretary of War 'that, as a lawyer, "'I supposed that I might be held personally for the sum.'" Of course, "as *a lawyer*," he knew that he was personally liable, and that was a good reason why he should pay it to the one to whom he was liable. But Gen. Butler, "as a lawyer," and as a man of common sense, well knew that, when Smith urged him "to pay over this money to the War Office or to the Treasury, and leave me to such remedy there as the Government may think fit," that the payment of the money to the War Office or to the Treasury, as Smith proposed, would relieve General Butler from all responsibility whatever. This appears in the record; it cannot be evaded; no subterfuge can dispose of it. This proposition of Smith to relieve General Butler, and to look to the Government for "such remedy as the Government may think fit to give," was made in writing March 26, 1864, was never withdrawn, and after seven months of subsequent and fruitless negotiation the letter of October 26, 1864, was written, saying, "You leave Mr. Smith no alternative but to commence an action."

Why, during those seven months between the proposition

and the commencement of this suit, did not General Butler pay over the gold to the Government, and thus relieve himself and leave Smith "to such remedy as the Government might think fit?"

There is no answer to this. Is it suggested that the Government would not receive the money? I assert deliberately, and after careful investigation, that during that whole time it was never offered to the Government; that they did not refuse to receive it; and I will peril the whole case upon the truth of this statement.

Instead of accepting this simple proposition of Smith's to pay over the gold to the Government, and thus relieve General Butler from all claim, the general kept the gold himself, devising new propositions, coupled with impossible conditions, and thus contrived to keep the gold from Mr. Smith and from the Government to the present hour.

This will appear from the written documents which follow.

This bold fact stands out, and refuses to be covered up, namely: That General Butler took this $50,000 in gold two years and nine months ago; that he has kept it ever since, and still keeps it, though Smith, as early as March 26, 1864, in writing, proposed that General Butler "pay over the "gold to the War Office, or to the Treasury, and leave me "to such remedy there as the Government may think fit;" which offer was never withdrawn, but remained open for seven full months, and until the 26th of October last, when the counsel, tired out by the evasions and subterfuges of impossible conditions, wrote: "You leave Mr. Smith no "alternative but to commence an action." General Butler still keeps the gold. Is it right that he should keep it?—Let us have that question settled. Officers in the army, from generals to corporals—the Government—the country—all have a lively interest in the disposition of this question. It will insist on being answered. No specious talk, in flurried debate, in an excited House, where not a man but the defendant himself knows a word of the evidence, can smother this question. It will rise up out of the smoke and insist on being answered.

But there are other grave matters in this case which cannot be slurred over. I especially invite your attention to the *dates* of this

## HISTORY.

The brilliant success of Admiral Farragut at New Orleans enabled General Butler to enter the city on the 1st of May, 1862. On the same day the general issued his proclamation, containing the following solemn pledge:

"*All the rights of property, of whatever kind, will be held*
" *inviolate, subject only to the laws of the United States.*
" *All the inhabitants are enjoined to pursue their usual*
" *avocations. All shops and places of amusement are to be*
" *kept open in the accustomed manner, and services are to*
" *be held in the churches and religious houses, as in times*
" *of profound peace.*"

Mr. Smith, in accordance with the proclamation, opened his banking house for business. On the 10th of May, 1862, General Butler took from him this $50,000 in gold. Not a word was said to the Government about it until the next July, when General Butler, by letter, now on file in the department, wrote to Mr. Chase, then Secretary of the Treasury, excusing himself for not sending the gold to the Treasury, on the ground that he was obliged to use it in paying his troops.

*This letter is dated July*, 1862, and is now on file in the department.

Subsequently Mr. Smith came on to Washington to ask the Government to repay him, having no suspicion that the gold had not been paid to the troops, as General Butler had written.

I was employed as counsel to present the claim, but was not able to give it attention till April. The Secretary of the Treasury examined the case and wrote as follows to the Secretary of War:

" Treasury Department,
April 2d, 1863.

" Sir,—Application has been made to this department
" for the repayment to Samuel Smith & Co. of $50,000
" alleged to have been seized by General Butler at New
" Orleans.

" An examination of the report made to this department
" by General Butler discloses the following facts: That

" $50,000 in coin in the possession of Smith & Co. was " seized by General Butler, *and by him appropriated to-* " *wards the pay of the Army*, and that the amount referred " to has *never reached the Treasury* of the United States. " Under these circumstances, the transaction being a mili- " tary one, the jurisdiction of the case rests exclusively with " the War Department."

Mr. Smith was a stranger to me, but he brought testimonials both from gentlemen of New Orleans and New York, of the very highest character. Those high testimonials have been subsequently confirmed in the most ample manner.

On the 11th of May, 1863, Mr. Smith's application was made to the War Department, and his long, full, and minute deposition of all the circumstances was there filed and referred to the Solicitor, who made no decision upon the case, but suggested that to get the money an act of Congress or resort to the Court of Claims might be necessary. Mr. Smith having gone back to New Orleans I awaited his return.

Meanwhile, learning that it was difficult to get money from the Treasury once paid in without an act of Congress, I prepared to apply to Congress for such act, and early in February, 1864, I wrote to the Hon. Henry G. Stebbins, member from New York, stating the case, and asking him to see Secretary Chase and find exactly how the money stood in the Treasury. Colonel Stebbins saw the Secretary, who gave the matter his prompt attention, and I was telegraphed to come to Washington. The Secretary then sent a clerk with me to go through the office of the Paymaster General and the other offices in which a record of the money must necessarily appear, to find on what account it stood. After a thorough investigation of the accounts of every paymaster through whom the money could have been paid out to the troops, no such payments could be found. And on the second day, after a fruitless re-examination, the officer in charge of the Paymaster General's office, suggested that I write to General Butler, then at Fortress Monroe, and learn through what paymaster he had paid out this $50,000 of gold to his troops; and he then turned to a young clerk in the office and said, (addressing him familiarly by name,) "You must know about this gold, as you were in New Orleans at the time?" The young man smiled and said that he did know about the gold, and gave us to understand that we were wasting our time—that General Butler never paid a dollar of the gold to his troops; that they were paid in paper, and there was no difficulty in tracing the paper from Washington to the paymasters, and from the paymasters to the troops. And thus was revealed to us for the first time the reason why we could not find how that gold got to the troops. The simple reason was, it never did get there; that was all. I had no personal acquaintance with General Butler, but through my hatred of the rebellion and belief that the General was of service to our cause I had been his defender, and hoping that there might be some possible mistake and that the General had not retained the money, I wrote him my first letter, as follows:

"February 29th, 1864.

"Dear Sir,—Samuel Smith, of Saratoga County, New York, formerly private banker in New Orleans, has a claim for $50,000 in gold used by General Butler in 1862 for payment of his troops in New Orleans. I write this in the Treasury Department with the letter of General Butler to the Secretary before me; it is dated July 2d, 1862. It was supposed by the Secretary that as the letter of General Butler stated that the money was used to pay the troops, that the credit for that $50,000 would be found in Paymaster-General's or Auditor's office. I have this day been over the accounts with the clerks, and no mention of the money appears. Will you do me the favor to say to what paymaster this money was given, and in what accounts this $50,000 should appear? I am the counsel of Mr. Smith, and the Paymaster-General suggests this as the quickest way to learn what paymaster had the money. Your letter of July 2d, 1862, only states the fact that the money was paid to your troops, without naming through what paymaster.

"The accounts of Hewitt, Sherman, Locke, and Usher have all been examined, and we find no account of it. Will you do me the favor to reply to this at my residence, No. 103 Fifth avenue, New York city, and much oblige,

"Yours very respectfully,

"Edwards Pierrepont.

"Major-General Butler."

Three days after I mentioned this matter to the Secretary of War, and learned to my surprise that General Butler claimed to retain the money, because "as a Lawyer *he* "*thought he might be held liable to Smith & Co., the* "*owners.*" I then addressed the following to the General:

"Treasury Department,
March 3, 1864.

"General,—When I had the honor to address you on the 29th ultimo, I was not as well advised as now. As counsel for Samuel Smith & Co., whose $50,000 in gold was taken in New Orleans, and which matter you had referred to the Treasury, together with all the papers, I have had the case examined, and have produced Mr. Smith and had his deposition with others taken here and filed. I had reached the point when I had supposed the money would be paid over, and the Secretary undertook to find to what credit it stood, and not being able to find out, at the suggestion of the Paymaster-General, I wrote to you.

"Now I have just learned from the Secretary of War more about the matter. Will you do me the favor to inform me who has the money, and to whom, in your judgment, I ought to look for it, and to whom it rightfully belongs?

"I am, very respectfully, your obedient servant,
"Edwards Pierrepont,
"16 Wall street, New York.

"Major-General Butler."

I waited two weeks and no reply came to either of my letters, and I sent the following:

"16 Wall Street, New York,
March 15, 1864.

"General,—Two weeks ago this day I wrote from Washington to learn where the $50,000 in gold taken from Samuel Smith & Co., New Orleans, now is. I wrote with yours of July 2, 1862, directed to the Secretary of the Treasury, before me, in which you speak of this gold; the letter is now on file with the report of Governor Shipley and others. I am Samuel Smith's counsel. Will you do me the favor to say what was the disposition of Mr. Smith's gold, where it is, and to whom, in your judgment, it rightly belongs?

"I also addressed you a second letter on the same subject. As I have no reply from either, I fear that you may not have received them.

"To avoid accident, I will send this in duplicate, and very respectfully await your reply.

"Ever your obedient servant,

"EDWARDS PIERREPONT,

"Counsel for Samuel Smith.

"Major-General BUTLER."

By accident I met an earnest supporter of the Government, a brave and well known public man, who was on his way to Fortress Monroe. I wrote a few words upon my card, and asked him to deliver it to General Butler.

On the 26th of March, 1864, I was honored with a reply commencing thus:

"HEADQ'RS DEP'T VIRGINIA AND NORTH CAROLINA,
Fortress Monroe, March 21, 1864.

"EDWARDS PIERREPONT, Esq.:

"I am in receipt of your letter in regard to the money alleged to be of Samuel Smith & Co., bankers, at New Orleans, up to the time of the capture of that city by the United States forces. As you are aware, I am in the field, and have, therefore, no books or papers with me relating to ormer transactions, and was obliged to wait until I had examined some memoranda before I could make as full an answer as I could wish. This must be my apology for the delay in answering your letters. I am now without date and amounts, but the facts and the order of sequence I am quite sure will be without mistake."

* * * * * * * *

This letter is very long, and is all published in the General's congressional defence, and charges Smith with having concealed the money, changed his books, &c., but admitting that he, the general, has not paid it over to the Government. Mr. Smith's books are all open; any one can look at them, and they will show for themselves; and Mr. Smith assures me that there is no foundation whatever for the statements about erasures and entries of "tin, &c.;" that a daily blotter used by an eccentric clerk had the word "tin" upon it, which was a cant word for "cash" used by the clerk on his daily blotter, but that there is no such thing in the books, but it is entered "cash" in the usual way; and that the books now existing prove it, and that this very thing was explained to General Butler at the time, in New Orleans.

Wishing to relieve General Butler of all responsibility in *longer* keeping my clients' money, and urgent to get the gold into the Treasury in ample time to get a bill through Congress, if necessary, before adjournment, I forthwith wrote:

"16 Wall street, New York,
March 26, 1864.

"My Dear General,—I am very truly obliged by your satisfactory letter received this hour. It fully explains the delay by which I have been a little annoyed. Pardon this suggestion; *why not pay over the money to the War Office or to the Treasury, and leave me to such remedy there as the Government may think fit?*

"*They now say the money is not in their hands.* Please let me hear upon this.

"Very truly yours,
"Edwards Pierrepont.

"Major-General Butler."

No imaginable excuse for non-compliance with this proposition has been offered. No *honest* excuse can ever be offered. Compliance was a release to General Butler from all claims whatsoever, and the General well knew it. We did not ask that it be paid to Smith, the owner, but simply to the Government. The General, instead of accepting the simple proposition, comes back with the following evasive reply:

"Headq'rs Dep't Virginia and North Carolina,
Fort Monroe, March 28, 1864.

"Dear Sir,—Your note of the 26th instant is received, and I am glad to be able to answer it speedily. I am much obliged for your suggestions. When I settled my accounts at the War Office, the question of what shall be done with this money of Samuel Smith & Co., came under discussion, and I then said to the Secretary of War, that as a lawyer, I supposed that I might be held personally for the sum, and that if he would give me an order to pay over the money to the War Office in such form to release me from the responsibility if hereafter called upon by Smith & Co., I should be glad to pay the money over. He doubted whether this could be done, and suggested the money might lie in my hands until the Department was called upon for it, and that a proper memorandum should be put on file, so that Smith & Co.'s rights, if they had any, should be preserved as well as my own. There is no difficulty in dealing with the money now in the same way.

"If the War Department directs an order to me to pay the money either into the Treasury or contingent fund of the Department, and Smith & Co., acting under your advice, will give me a memorandum stating that such payment shall relieve me from personal responsibility, I will give a draft for the amount on the Assistant Treasurer of the United States that will be honored at once.

"I think it but right, however, that my first letter to you stating the facts of the capture of the money should be laid before the War Department for its information before any order is made on the subject, transferring the funds to Smith & Co.

"I have the honor to be, very respectfully, your obedient servant,

"Benj. F. Butler,
"Major-General Commanding."

Hoping that I could hold him to his own suggestion in some form, I replied as follows:

"16 Wall Street, New York, April 1, 1864.

"My Dear General,—I am very glad to receive your letter of the 28th of March. I am not one of your enemies. That matter will now be adjusted, and I will write you some statement of facts of which it is evident you are not apprised. Immediately after the seizure of the gold, Smith came here; he was born in Saratoga county, where his mother now lives, and he has been with her here, and in Washington, most of the time since.

"He employed Senator Reverdy Johnson and myself as his counsel; as the younger man, I have been the more active. The report of the commissioners which you appointed clearly established beyond all controversy that the gold belonged to Smith. The commissioners so report; and the evidence returned with the report abundantly established the conclusion.

"These papers, with your letter of July 2, 1862, are now in the Treasury Department, and I have complete copies of them all. I took Mr. Smith to Washington, and his deposition was taken at great length, and is now on file with the other papers. Mr. Smith is a Yankee, born of a Yankee, bred a Yankee, has taken the oath of allegiance, and is as true and loyal as you or I. He has not been in Canada at all; he tried, in the fright and terror which prevailed in New Orleans, to save his property in part. Dr. Mercer, who acted on the commission, is now here. I am truly glad that this matter is about to be adjusted. Not every one who has been in the case has the same desire to have it quietly settled as I have. My own view about the case is this: I think it quite clear that you could not successfully resist a suit in New York brought by Smith to recover whatever damages he can prove. *I think the true way to settle it is for you to pay Smith and take a release, with the assent of the War Department. If you agree with me I will see that it is done in such a way as you shall say is liberal and just. I await your reply.*

"Ever truly yours,

"EDWARDS PIERREPONT.

"Major-General BUTLER."

To this I received the following still more evasive reply:

"April 4, 1864.

"My Dear Sir: *I can only repeat my offer that whenever the War Department will order the money paid over to your client, and he shall give me a release*, my draft for the amount will be forwarded. I am glad to hear that Mr. Smith is loyal. His conversion I trust is sincere. For yourself, I thank you for your expressions of kindness and confidence, and while they are very gratifying indeed to one who has been so much maligned as I have been, yet you will see in this transaction I have so lived as to defy my enemies. Allow me, my dear sir, further to say that, '*Ex uno disce omnes.*' For a while you will confess to yourself that you doubted my action in this business. I am as willing that every act of my official life shall be as thoroughly investigated as this may be. Therefore you will see that, while I am obliged for the friendly feeling which prompted you to desire the case 'quietly settled,' still if those who desired otherwise had had their way I should have been as well pleased, because conscious of having endeavored to do my duty. An attack upon me in this case would have failed, and thus answered a thousand others to which no reply can ever be otherwise made. Upon the point of law which you suggest, pardon me if I differ with a lawyer so distinguished as yourself. I do not believe that a military commander in a captured city, taking money (contraband of war) which might be used against that officer's army, from an *alien enemy*, can be held liable for the capture as a trespass for the tort for not returning upon demand which might sustain trover after the enemy became a friend and capacitated to sue. I am inclined that having paid the money to his Government would answer the demand. *It was to avoid this after-question, however, (I had no doubt on the first,) that I hesitated to pay the money to the Government.* Still I am rusty at the law, and my opinions are not now, if they ever were, worth much.

"Yours truly,

"B. F. BUTLER."

We did not expect *the War Department to order General Butler* to pay Smith; we asked that Gen. Butler *pay the* Treasury or the War Department, which he would not do, but replied by a proposition *to pay Smith*, coupled with conditions, which he well knew the War Department could not comply with. The General says at the end of the above Letter, "IT WAS TO AVOID THIS AFTER QUESTION, THAT I HESITATED TO PAY THE MONEY TO THE GOVERNMENT."

To avoid *something*, the General has "hesitated *to pay the money to the Government*" to this very hour.

He has *hesitated* for two years and nine months, and still *hesitates*; he also *hesitates* to pay it over to Smith & Co., the owners; he *does not hesitate* to keep every dollar of this Gold himself.

I deliberately charge that neither the Secretary of the Treasury or the Secretary of War ever refused to accept this money from General Butler; that he did not take it or retain it by the order, or at the request of any Secretary of the Treasury or of War. It was the General that "hesitated to pay the money over to the Government" and not the Government that "*hesitated* to receive it. The Secretaries are both living. Let the General call upon them in this matter.

I now call your attention to my reply to the above, and which reply the General carefully suppresses—in his published defence. Why it was suppressed will be apparent:

NEW YORK, 16 Wall street,
May 4, 1864.

" Major-Gen. BUTLER :

"Dear Sir,—Since your proposition to pay over to Smith & Co. the $50,000 upon order from the Secretary of War. I have seen the Secretary, and have just returned from Washington. The Secretary first thought that there was no objection, but upon consultation with Mr. Whiting, he concluded *that as the money never came to the War Department, and as it was never taken by any order of the Department, and as General Butler had retained it on the ground that he might be personally liable if he paid it over; the Department would take no action whatever as to the payment of the money.* I think the Department acted wisely. I do not see what business the Department has with the money *which you hold and not they, and which they have never had, and which theg never authorized to be taken* Smith was with me ; the Smiths both live in Ballston's Spa, N. Y., where they were born ; they long since took the Oath of Allegiance, the amnesty oath, and are ready to take any others required—they are as loyal as you or I. I propose this ; send your draft for the money to any one in New York in whom you trust, to be paid over on full release. Or let any one appear for you, and you may have an amicable suit in any Court in New York, United States Court or State Court, as you please.

" This is not a hostile but a friendly proposition, as any one will tell you. Otherwise, you force me to a suit by long publications in the newspapers, as you are not resident.

" I await your reply, and am

Truly yours,

" EDWARDS PIERREPONT."

P. S. June 4.—"I retained the above, because the General was in the Field ; but your letter of last evening in the New York Express, causes me to hope for an answer to this.

Yours, truly,

" E. P."

The General read this letter, as his replies of October 8 and 28, both prove, but he still " *hesitated* " to part with the Gold! He " hesitated" to accept any possible practicable proposition or suggestion which would relieve him of the gold. He " hesitated" to answer this letter until the 8th of the next October, and then wrote making excuses for delay and repeating his impracticable propositions. My courtesy, which I had tried to have delicate, as well as patient, grew a little weary, and I wrote the following: —"Enclosing a Summons."

16 WALL STREET,
October 26, 1864.

"My Dear Sir,—You leave Mr. Smith no alternative but to commence an action. It is not necessary there be any publications in the papers if you will authorize any attorney to appear for you, but otherwise it is necessary.

I do not wish any publication unless you wish it. Please let me know your attorney at once, if you have one here.

Truly, EDWARDS PIERREPONT.

Major-General BUTLER.

The following is his reply:

HEADQUARTERS NEAR VARNA,
October 28, 1864.

My Dear Sir,—Your note inclosing the summons and complaint in the case of Mr. Smith and Brother was received last evening in the field. I hasten to answer.

Although not a resident of New York or amenable to the jurisdictions of her Courts, so that a summons could hardly bring me in, yet I shall at once acknowledge service and instruct my attorney, John K. Hackett, Esq., to make answer. Having done this, I shall rely on your courtesy to allow me a little time to go to Washington to make the following disposition of the cause. When you desired me to assent to a friendly suit I could make no answer to the proposition, because as an official I could do nothing in any way to compromise the rights of the United States. Now, however, your proceeding *in invitum* leaves me in a different situation, because, although I am acknowledging service, still as I must come to New York and can hardly travel *incog.*, you could obtain service, and therefore without prejudice a suit may be considered fairly begun.

I will now apply to the War Department, and ask the Government to assume the defence; if that is done, then I have no further interest in the matter; if not, then I am at liberty to arrange with your client, or contest the suit as I choose, and am left free to negotiate about a matter in which I can have no personal interest except to save myself from cost. So soon, therefore, as I can get away, which I hope to be in a few days, I will make answer, or will meet you as you prefer, and be able to state exactly my position on this subject. Of course, the suit, if it goes forward, will be removed into the Courts of the United States. You will not need to be told that these suggestions do not proceed from any desire to delay your clients; but, in fact, to further their interest, if they have any. You will please answer me at once whether this course will meet your concurrence.

As to the publication, I beg leave to repeat to you that I can have no objection to any person knowing every fact connected with this transaction. The most exaggerated stories have been told about it privately, from which I am suffering; but what can I do about it that I have not done.

Respectfully,

BENJ. F. BUTLER,
Major-General.

HON. EDWARDS PIERREPONT.

I replied as follows:

16 WALL STREET,
November 2, 1864.

My Dear General,—Yours received, and satisfactory. You have been a general since you were a lawyer, and when you speak of jurisdiction I think you have not read our recent statute.

We have a way to get *jurisdiction* not like the old way; but that is no matter. I will show you when we meet. Your proposition is satisfactory, and I shall confer with your attorney.

I send you my speech.

Yours,

EDWARDS PIERREPONT.

Major-General BUTLER.

This reply is published in the Globe, *before* the letter to which it relates—any one who can read, will see that the words "yours received and satisfactory" relates to Gen. Butler's attorney, and to the future conduct of the suit, and yet it being inserted before the letter of Gen. Butler, has led the newspapers to say in their comments that I had expressed myself perfectly satisfied with the General's course about the gold. The whole defence before the House, partakes of the same character. It seems got up for effect upon an excited house in an excited hour, when Smith had no advocate, and no hearing.

The action being commenced, the General then hesitated about his answer, and commenced delays by a motion to remove the cause out of the State Court, which holds a term monthly, to the United States Court, which has but two terms for the trial of civil causes in an entire year.

On the 6th of November, I received a friendly note from the General, expressing a desire to see me at the Hoffman house in New York—on the 8th I called—we soon reached the matter of the gold. The General said, that if the Government did not assume the defence, he would adjust the case fairly. I met him once afterwards; he then said that he was going direct to Washington, that he would see the Secretary of War, and have the matter settled up. I was quite satisfied, and parted with the General in the full belief that tardy justice was about to be done to my client.

The General departed for Washington on Tuesday, November 15th, and on Thursday morning, under the head of telegraphic news from Washington, appeared the following:

(*From the Tribune.*)

GEN. BUTLER'S GOLD.

The copperhead attachment for General Butler's New Orleans gold will have to penetrate the vaults of the United States Treasury before it will be forthcoming, every dollar being in the keeping of that department.

(*From the Times.*)

THAT GOLD.

Concerning the attachment applied for against General Butler, in New York, on behalf of the parties in New Orleans, to recover $60,000 in gold, seized by General Butler in that city, it is proper to say that the gold referred to is in the Treasury of the United States, and that the plaintiffs must seek redress, if they feel aggrieved, against the government, and not General Butler.

(*From the Herald.*)

THE ATTACHMENT AGAINST GENERAL BUTLER.

The parties who have brought suit in New Orleans against General Butler for gold seized in New Orleans, will find that it is the government, and not the individual, they have a claim against. The gold in question was condemned by a military commission *as the proceeds of the robbery of the United States Mint in New Orleans*, and was accounted for to the War Department, in whose custody it has since been. General Butler has at all times been ready to pay over the money claimed whenever an order of the War Department should be presented.

And on the following morning, in the Tribune, appeared this also:

*Special Despatch to The N. Y. Tribune.*

WASHINGTON, Thursday, Nov. 17, 1864.

THE WAR OFFICE OFFERED TO GENERAL BUTLER.

"The physical prostration of Secretary Stanton rendering his withdrawal from the War Office inevitable, the President, according to a wide-spread and strongly fortified desire, tendered the position to Gen. Butler yesterday in person. It is understood that the general, for the present at least, declined the honor, and left for more active operations at the front."

Mr. Smith's gold hopes drew dim. If this was the kind of settlement the general intended to make, we felt that we had been a little "*humbugged.*" The world was given to understand that this Smith was a "copperhead," bringing an outrageous suit against General Butler for gold of which Smith had robbed the United States Mint, and which the General had restored to the vaults of the United States Treasury. It would also appear that this worthy act was appreciated, as "the President had tendered the office of Secretary of War to General Butler *in person*"—a rough kind of "settlement" that, Smith thought. His gold, the toil of years, had been taken away by force, and now it was publicly charged that "the gold was the proceeds of a robbery of the United States Mint."

I was in Washington the next day, and found that not a dollar of the money had been paid over, and that the whole fabrication, from the beginning down to the statement that "the President yesterday tendered the position of Secretary of War to General Butler in person," was exactly what Lieut. General Grant and Admiral Porter publicly stated of Butler's Fort Fisher Report.

The motion to remove the cause was pending. I applied to General Butler's very capable and honorable counsel, Mr. Hackett, to get the motion adjourned, and twice I got it adjourned. My object was to give ample time to have these libels upon Mr. Smith retracted. No corrections were

2

made. I sent for Mr. Smith, and told him to make a full statement of the facts—such as he could swear to—such as would stand every test in future.

No one who knows Mr. Smith will doubt his statements, whether under oath or not. He is a man of established character, well known.

He made an affidavit, which was read in Court. I made a few remarks—not quite so courteous as my letters, which were read before Congress. General Butler lost his motion.

This is the affidavit:

"Court of Common Pleas for the City and County of New York.

"Samuel Smith and Andrew W. Smith *vs.* Benjamin F. Butler.

"City and County of New York, ss.:

"Samuel Smith, one of the plaintiffs above named, being duly sworn on solemn oath, deposes and says:

"That some twenty years ago he left the county of Saratoga, in this State, where he was born, and where his mother still resides, and went to New Orleans, without any means but youth and hope, to seek for better fortune. By severe economy, constant toil, and the unremitting industry of long years, he and his brother Andrew together, succeeded in acquiring a considerable property, and they became extensively engaged in the business of private banking. Their very business compelled them to make constant advances of money on Southern credits. When the war broke out they were extended, and it was not possible for them to collect in their claims without much delay. The State of Louisiana seceded—deponent opposed the secession, and quietly remained to liquidate his affairs, and save what he could. It is easy for those who were safe in the North to talk bravely about their patriotism, and to boast of what they would have done; but had such been where we were they might have thought differently.

"On the 24th of April, 1862, news came that Admiral Farragut had passed the lower forts. The greatest consternation prevailed. All who had any money wished to conceal it. The fear was of the wild mob and the soldiery, in case the city should be given up to pillage. Deponent had about sixty thousand dollars in gold coin in his safe, which he had been collecting together, and which he had hoped to save. In this frightful consternation, deponent took $54,000 of the gold coin and secreted it in the air cells around his safe, and left about $6,000 of his own in the safe, besides a small amount belonging to some of his customers. Admiral Farragut's success left New Orleans at his mercy, and General Butler entered the city on the 1st of May, and the rebel soldiery fled, and there was no pillage of the town. Forthwith General Butler issued his proclamation, dated May 1, 1862, and directed every man to return to his business, and promising the fullest protection, and expressed himself in these words: '*All the rights of property, of whatever kind, will be held inviolate, subject only to the laws of the United States. All the inhabitants are enjoined to pursue their usual avocations. All shops and places of amusement are to be kept open in the accustomed manner, and services are to be held in the churches and religious houses, as in times of profound peace.*' Deponent did not suppose that this solemn proclamation by a general of the United States was intended as a delusion and a snare, and opened his banking house in the fullest confidence that the general would not violate his plighted faith. The secreted coin could not be reached without tearing down a wall of masonry, and deponent being unwilling to excite notice by tearing down a heavy brick wall and withdrawing the coin, when the city was in such a fearful state, let it remain for a few days to await events. General Butler soon began to examine into the affairs of banks, bankers, and men supposed to have money, for what public end no one could understand.

"On the 10th of May General Butler ordered deponent to open his safe, which he did; but the general finding but six thousand dollars in coin in the safe, while deponent's books showed sixty thousand dollars in hand, demanded the concealed coin, which deponent refused to give up, telling Gen. Butler that it was concealed, and the object of the concealment, but declining to reveal the place where it was secreted. The general then ordered deponent to prison, and threatened to confine him in Fort Jackson until he revealed the place of concealment. Deponent was powerless, without the protection of law, and at the mercy of despotic force. After being imprisoned in the manner above described, deponent revealed the place where the gold was secreted. General Butler tore down the masonry, and carried off the fifty-four thousand dollars in gold, besides the money in the safe, and after a few days he returned to deponent the six thousand left in the safe, and four thousand dollars of the concealed coin, keeping fifty thousand dollars in gold, which he has retained from deponent to this hour. The general then let deponent go, despoiled of his hard-earned property, and with his business broken up and destroyed, and now when deponent seeks in a lawful way to obtain redress, he is met with these false telegrams from Washington. The statement that 'this gold was condemned by a military commission as the proceeds of the robbery of the United States Mint at New Orleans' is without a shadow of truth, is utterly malicious, and is in every syllable basely false. Every dollar of it belonged to the plaintiff. It was the proceeds of long and patient toil; not a penny of it ever belonged to the mint or to any confederate state office or department thereof, and the military commission so found; and the one who ordered that false telegram sent knew or ought to have known it. Deponent makes this affidavit with a true copy of that commission and report before him. That commission was composed of three able and upright men—Governor Shipley, Hon. Thos. J. Durant, and Dr. Mercer—and their report was made in June, 1862, and proves the shameless falsity of these slanderous telegrams.

"Deponent took the oath of allegiance—the amnesty oath—and is as true and loyal a man as he who by military force has taken away deponent's property. Deponent respectfully submits that this false charge about a copperhead attachment, and these false and slanderous charges that deponent's gold 'is the proceeds of a robbery of the United States Mint,' published in the newspapers through telegrams from Washington while General Butler was there, and for the purpose of deceiving the public, and of prejudicing their mind, before the trial of the cause (which cause had been legitimately commenced under the order of this court), deserved the rebuke and severest condemnation of every judge and right-thinking man in this community.

* * * * * * *

* * * * * * * *

(Signed) SAM SMITH.

Sworn to this 29th of November, 1864, before me, Fred. Smyth, Notary Public, New York.

The suit was commenced in October, 1864. Did the General then propose to pay the money into Court or to the Government? Not a bit of it. But contriving a new devise by which to retain the money in his own hands, he wrote to the Solicitor of the War Department the following very *persuasive* letter:

HEADQ'RS DEP'T VIRGINIA AND NORTH CAROLINA,
FORTRESS MONROE, VA., *November* 28, 1864.

MY DEAR WHITING,—I inclose herewith to you a note to the Secretary of War, in relation to the matter of Samuel Smith & Co., bankers at New Orleans.

*I think it a clear case for a test question, and hope the Government will defend it.* Please bring the paper to the notice of the Secretary, and get his permission to allow me to publish the note in my own justification.

Although somewhat thick-skinned to newspaper attacks, yet some of my good and true friends are writing me that I ought to explain the facts, and I know no better way to do so than by such publication.

If I may rely upon those friendly relations which exist between us, upon you to procure this to be done, you will add another to the many obligations under which I am to yourself.

By the by, why do you not come to the "front" and see how war is actuully carried on? I will give you a "plate and a blanket."

Yours, truly, BENJ. F. BUTLER,
*Major-General.*

Hon. WILLIAM WHITING, *Solicitor of the War Department.*

The avowed object of this letter was to get the Government to defend the suit.

He says: "*I think it is a clear case for a test question, and hope the Government will defend it.*"

A test of what? and why did he wish the Government to defend it?

It seems that he wished, not only that the Government should defend the suit, but that the Government should indemnify him also.

The Government *refused*, and replied to him as follows:

WAR DEPARTMENT, WASHINGTON CITY,
*December* 6, 1864.

GENERAL,—I am instructed by the Secretary of War to inform you—

*First.*—That your communication dated at Fortress Monroe, November 28, and addressed to him in relation to the claim of Samuel Tmith & Co. against you, was referred to the Judge Advocate General for opinion and report on the question of indemnity you ask for.

Upon that reference, the Judge Advocate General reports:

"*The question of indemnification cannot be determined at this stage of the proceedings. Should there be a judgment against the applicant his rights to be indemnified against it will depend upon the character of his conduct, considered in all its bearings, which has given rise to the suit.* This will be best understood when examined in the light of the testimony which will be produced on the trial. If the applicant acted within the scope of his power, fairly interpreted, his claims to protection against the results of this suit should be allowed. *The fact that he has retained the gold seized and now holds it, subject to the order of the Government, is not considered as affecting the right obligation involved.*"

This report is approved, and will govern the action of the Department upon your request for indemnity.

*Second.*—In relation to your request for leave to publish your letter to the Secretary of War, the Secretary directs me to say that no objection is made by the Department to your publication of any statement in regard to the claim of Smith & Co., which you may deem essential for your vindication.

*Third.*—In reference to the information given by you to tne Department, a copy of your memorandum in relation to the gold of Smith & Co., seized by you, filed with your accounts and vouchers in the War Department, is hereto annexed.

I am, general, very respectfully, yaur obedient servant,

E. D. Townsend,

*Assistant Adjutant General.*

To Major-General B. F. Butler.

The Government *declined* to aid the General in longer keeping Smith's gold; and yet the General still holds on to it. Parting with $50,000 of gold, long kept, seems to be attended with reluctance;—perhaps it is natural. Take $50,000 of another man's gold—keep it two years and nine months without giving security to any one—use it as your own; let it rise to 285, and a natural affection springs up for the increasing treasure not to be severed without a pang; natural affections are to be respected; but Mr. Smith has also a certain lingering attachment to that gold—the honest earnings of many long and weary years. Mr. Smith is not a rebel; he is a true Northern man; when a boy he went from Saratoga county down to New Orleans to better his humble fortune; he opposed secession with all his power; when it came, he did as he best could, gathered in something of his property, put it into gold, hoping to save it, and to reach his old home where his mother still lives.

The next step in this history was Gen. Butler's defence before Congress, which we have already reviewed.

I understood Gen. Butler to suggest, in his defence, that gold was not above par in July, 1862, when it was said he paid it to his troops. Gen. Butler's letter to the Secretary of the Treasury, in which he states that he shall pay the gold to the troops, reached Washington about the 19th of July. Gold was then 20 per cent. above par; on the 10th it was 18, and as early as the 3d it was over 10 per cent. premium. And Gen. Butler's letter of July, now with the Secretary, shows that he then knew that gold was more valuable than paper. Since Gen. Butler has had this gold it has sold as high as 285. Whether the General sold it at these prices, or whether he has kept this identical gold, we know not, but we are willing to take the chances of his shrewdness and to receive exactly the proceeds. I suspect that the Government will not like to establish the precedent that a General can seize another man's gold and keep it himself, on any pretext or for any private speculations.

The grievances charged in this case are these:

*First.*—That in violation of his proclamation and without authority of law, Gen. Butler took $50,000 in gold from Smith & Co., in New Orleans.

*Second.*—That this gold was the property of Smith & Co., acquired by honest industry.

*Third.*—That Smith & Co. were northern men, engaged as bankers in New Orleans, La. Their business was extended, their credits in that State of necessity were long. They opposed secession with all their power, and when secession came upon them they tried to gather in their property as best they could; That, being northern men, they were more liable to suspicion, and were, of course, compelled to be very circumspect. That when a safe opportunity offered, they gladly took the oath of allegiance, and the amnesty oath also. That they concealed the gold to keep it from the mob, which it was supposed would pillage the city if Admiral Farragut passed the forts, and this concealment was made a pretext for seizing the gold by Gen. Butler.

*Fourth.*—That Gen. Butler has not paid out this gold to his troops, but has retained it. (It is quite likely that Gen. Butler left the gold for a time in the safe keeping of a paymaster; but the *point is*, that the gold was returned to the General and not paid out to the troops.

*Fifth.*—That Gen. Butler did not take the gold, nor has he retained the gold, by any order, authority, or direction of the Secretary of the Treasury or of War, and that he did not pay it over to the Government as Mr. Smith requ sted.

*Sixth.*—That so gross was the wrong to Smith & Co., and so clearly were they entitled to this money, that even General Butler's own Commissioners found that Smith & Co. were the owners, and wrote to the General, advising a restoration of the money, which has never yet been restored.

*Seventh.*—That Gen. Butler took this gold on the 10th of May, 1862, and did not report it to the War Department until February of the following year; and then reported that Smith & Co. were "*active rebels*," and "hesitated" to pay it over to the Government, lest these "rebels" sue him; to whom, "*as a lawyer*," he thought he might be liable!

Some years ago a gentleman, eminent for his piety, travelling on the Upper Nile, and lingering too late to gather relics from the shores of that ancient river, was seized by Arabs; and, to save his life, was compelled to outwardly adopt the religion of Mahomet. When he escaped to a christian land he hastened to worship with more grateful devotion than before at the shrine of The Savior. Did not God forgive him?!

Many a loyal man, lingering on the banks of the Mississippi to gather in his effects, was caught unawares and obliged to seemingly acquiesce in that hated rule. My client was one. At the earliest safe hour he returned to the home of his youth and to renewed allegiance to the government of his love.

'*Tis pitiful*, to hear men whose religion and whose patriotism has not been tried, talk so harshly of every fellow-man who, by temporary and seeming acquiescence, saved himself and his children from martyrdom.

When I foresee the bloody troubles through which our country has yet to pass; when I perceive the increasing difficulty of recruiting the armies which will surely be needed; when I see a General, fretted at the loss of power, trying by farewell order and by public speech, to make our soldiers believe that the best Generals will but lead them to uselessly bloody graves, and thus discouraging our brave and saddened people; and when I see this same General, through an honest member, palm off upon an honest House what I know to be a sham, I feel impelled by something higher than personal considerations to raise my voice against it.

The General, in his communication with the Secretary of War, excused himself for not paying over the money to the Government, on the ground that, "*as a lawyer*," he thought he might be held personally liable, in a Court of Justice, to Smith & Co., who, as he wrote the Secretary, "were active rebels." Gen. Butler, "*as a lawyer*," knew that "active rebels" could not sue in our Courts. Either he did not believe that Smith & Co. were "active rebels," or his excuse for not paying the money to the Government, through fear of recovery by them, was a sham. The next device to retain the money (after Smith proposed "that "he pay the money over to the Treasury, or the War De-"partment, and leave him to such remedy there as the "Government might think fit"), was to require an "ORDER" from the War Department. The General knew that the Government could not give "*Orders*" about every trespass, or other violation of municipal law, which every officer might commit. That would be assuming that the act was lawful. The Government *receive* money, or other property, turned over to it by any of its officers, but it will not, and it cannot make "*Orders*" about it, which assume that the act was either right or wrong. There has been no time in which Gen. Butler could not have turned over this money to the Government, as he well knows. *Why does he keep the Gold?*

These facts cannot be denied; namely: That without the least authority of law Gen. Butler took this gold and has kept it two years and nine months and still keeps it;

That Gen. Butler's own commissioners found that the money belonged to Smith & Co., and desired to restore it;

That Mr. Smith supposing that Gen. Butler had paid the gold to his troops, as indicated by the general's letter, applied to the Treasury and found, to his surprise, that Gen. Butler had the gold;

That forthwith Mr. Smith, by his counsel, proposed in writing to Gen. Butler that he pay the money over to the Treasury or to the War Department *and leave Mr. Smith to such remedy as the Government might think fit to give him.*

That the General (to use his own words) "*hesitated*" to pay it to the Government and refused to pay it to the owner, and by various devises has contrived to retain it to this time, and without security either to the Government or to Mr. Smith, and with the full use of this $50,000 of gold during a period of two years and nine months;

Upon these facts an honest and intelligent people will pass a just judgment.

Each man in his sphere, however narrow or extended, will find that his fellow men, (whether he will or no) weigh his character and his abilities often; and unconsciously stamp him with their estimate, and that the average resultant of these frequent estimates *is just.*

If General Butler shall finally succeed in keeping Mr. Smith's gold to himself, he will find it an uncomfortable possession; and as his showy carriage rolls by, his honest townsmen will look up, and think of the boy who from Saratoga county went down to New Orleans in search of better fortune, and whose $50,000 in gold, the proceeds of patient toil, and the industry of long years, was taken from him by General Butler. And some humble, pious neighbor may say to the rich general:

"Your gold and silver is cankered; and the rust of them "shall be a witness against you, andshall eat your flesh as "it were fire."

Gen. Butler still keeps the gold, or the proceeds at 285, if he sold at the highest price.

Is IT RIGHT? That is the question—and I am truly yours

EDWARDS PIERREPONT,

*Counsel for Saml. Smith & Co.*

New York, February 10th, 1865.

www.ingramcontent.com/pod-product-compliance
Lightning Source LLC
LaVergne TN
LVHW011627120826
845150LV00012B/2349